RAND NATIONAL DEFENSE RESEARCH INSTITUTE

Supporting Persistent and Networked Special Operations Forces (SOF) Operations

Insights from Forward-Deployed SOF Personnel

Derek Eaton, Angela O'Mahony, Thomas S. Szayna, William Welser IV

Prepared for United States Special Operations Command

For more information on this publication, visit www.rand.org/t/RR1333

Library of Congress Cataloging-in-Publication Data
ISBN: 978-0-8330-9254-0

Published by the RAND Corporation, Santa Monica, Calif.
© Copyright 2017 RAND Corporation

RAND® is a registered trademark.

Support RAND
Make a tax-deductible charitable contribution at
www.rand.org/giving/contribute

www.rand.org

Preface

U.S. Special Operations Command's (USSOCOM's) mission is to synchronize the planning of special operations and to provide special operations forces (SOF) to support persistent, networked, and distributed operations. To do so, USSOCOM is developing a synchronized network of people and technology to provide sustained, persistent, SOF-specific capabilities and capacities and increased persistent forward-deployed presence to support the geographic combatant commands in the execution of their theater campaign plans. The primary focus of this network is phase 0 and phase 1 activities designed to shape perceptions, build partners' capabilities, and deter conflict. Understanding the day-to-day phase 0 and phase 1 operational activities of forward-deployed SOF personnel and the factors that critically influence the outcomes of their tactical operations can help shape USSOCOM efforts to prepare its personnel to support geographic combatant commands in the execution of their theater campaign plans, work with and leverage critical interagency partners, and strengthen partnerships with like-minded allies. To gain insight into the day-to-day operational activities of forward-deployed SOF personnel, USSOCOM asked the RAND Corporation to identify key operational challenges that forward-deployed SOF personnel have encountered and to assess whether these operational difficulties can be addressed through the implementation of persistent, networked, and distributed operations. This research was conducted in 2013 and 2014, but the issues and potential solutions identified here remain relevant.

This research was sponsored by USSOCOM and conducted within the International Security and Defense Policy Center of the RAND National Defense Research Institute, a federally funded research and development center sponsored by the Office of the Secretary of Defense, the Joint Staff, the Unified Combatant Commands, the Navy, the Marine Corps, the defense agencies, and the defense Intelligence Community.

For more information on the RAND International Security and Defense Policy Center, see www.rand.org/nsrd/ndri/centers/isdp or contact the director (contact informa-tion is provided on the web page).

Contents

Figures

U.S. strategic goals. For phase 0 and phase 1 missions in which SOF personnel build on the work done by previously deployed personnel, lack of detailed knowledge of past operations and future planned operations can undermine the long-term trajectory and ultimate achievement of geographic combatant commander (GCC) objectives.

Third, SOF personnel often found navigating the administrative complexity of contracts, funding procedures, and foreign disclosure and vetting processes challenging. Administrative complexity posed two key problems for SOF personnel. First, it took time away from other tasks that SOF personnel could have been undertaking. For small deployed teams in which each team member is responsible for multiple tasks, increased administrative burdens were seen as a significant erosion of available team capacity. Second, for teams that were unaware of the length of time administrative procedures would take, administrative complexity posed delays that forced teams to revise, truncate, or cancel planned operations.

Although SOF personnel often were able to mitigate the adverse operational consequences posed by poor unity and continuity of effort and administrative complexity, the time and resource burdens that these operational challenges created and the poor situational awareness they engendered risk degrading teams' effectiveness in current and future missions.

PND operations can provide opportunities to address the key operational challenges that forward-deployed SOF personnel experienced during phase 0 and phase 1 missions. However, these opportunities will depend crucially on how these operations are implemented. As the critical element in PND operations, enhanced TSOCs have the potential to greatly improve SOF effectiveness. Some improvements accruing to enhanced TSOCs will stem directly from the higher personnel numbers assigned and the consequent removal of constraints on the ability to engage in the full range of planning and coordination activities. But according to the SOF personnel who took part in our focus groups, the assignment of appropriately trained staff to the TSOCs for extended periods of time is essential in order to ensure that all the gains of more-robust TSOCs are realized. By *appropriately trained*, we are referring to personnel with a deep understanding of SOF operations and the regional knowledge of the area of operations. To ensure continuity, these personnel also need to remain in their posts for extended periods of time because there is no substitute for relationship-building with GCCs, embassies, and partner nations. In short, robust TSOCs are not just about more numbers but also about high-quality personnel.

Increased forward deployments also have the potential to enhance the impact of SOF activities. The effect can be substantial if the activities are coordinated with other U.S. efforts and build on prior SOF activities with partner forces. That implies good planning, information-sharing, and visibility into the activities that the services conduct and monitoring of progress toward clearly established goals. A similarly well-coordinated set of planning processes with partners can enhance the value of SOF activities.

Acknowledgments

We appreciate the support that personnel at U.S. Special Operations Command (USSOCOM) provided in the course of this research. Thomas McArthur and Troy S. Secor at USSOCOM were indispensable to the project by providing access to USSOCOM documentation. We thank COL Guy LeMire at the Naval Postgraduate School for facilitating our focus-group sessions. We are grateful to the special operations forces personnel at the Naval Postgraduate School for participating in our focus-group sessions. We are grateful to Linda Robinson and William Knarr for their astute and constructive feedback.

At RAND, Agnes Gereben Schaefer also contributed to this effort.

Abbreviations

AAR	after-action report
AFRICOM	U.S. Africa Command
BPC	building partner capacity
C2	command and control
CA	civil affairs
CME	civil–military engagement
CMSE	civil–military support element
COM	chief of mission
CP-GSO	Campaign Plan for Global Special Operations
FWD	forward
GCC	geographic combatant commander
GSN	global special operations forces network
HN	host nation
JCET	joint combined exchange training
JSOAD	joint special operations aviation detachment
MISO	military information support operations
MIST	military information support team
NSDD	national security decision directive
PN	partner nation
PND	persistent, networked, and distributed

SC	security cooperation
SDO/DATT	senior defense official/defense attaché
SITREP	situation report
SOC	special operations command
SOCAFRICA	Special Operations Command Africa
SOF	special operations forces
SOFLE	special operations forces liaison element
SOLO	special operations liaison officer
TSOC	theater special operations command
USSOCOM	U.S. Special Operations Command

CHAPTER ONE

Introduction

Persistent, Networked, and Distributed Special Operations

U.S. Special Operations Command's (USSOCOM's) mission is to synchronize the planning of special operations and to provide special operations forces (SOF) to "support persistent, networked and distributed Global Combatant Command operations."[1] This mission requires networked relationships with the geographic combatant commands, interagency partners, U.S. international partners, and U.S. national security decisionmakers to build a common understanding of shared threats, facilitate cooperation, and provide capabilities to address emerging threats (R. Thomas, 2017; USSOCOM, 2016, p. 14; Votel, 2015, pp. 3, 14; Votel, 2016, p. 1). The execution of persistent, networked, and distributed (PND) operations enables USSOCOM to conduct small-footprint persistent engagement at strategically important locations that integrate a network of partners. Persistent engagement helps nurture relationships to the "left of the bang" that build trust, increase understanding, facilitate stability, buy time to prevent conflict, and shape the environment for the use of short-notice direct action should it become necessary (R. Thomas, 2017, pp. 10–11; R. Thomas, 2016b, p. 4; Votel, 2015, p. 8). General Thomas highlighted the criticality of such operations when he stated that

> we must engage, not only where problems occur, but also in places critical to our vital national interests where no visible threat currently exists. Success in meeting these challenges demands unprecedented levels of trust, confidence, and understanding built through persistent engagement. (R. Thomas, 2016b, p. 4)[2]

---

[1] The USSOCOM commander, GEN Raymond A. Thomas, reiterated the importance of this mission when he told Congress that "it is imperative we continue to provide the most highly trained and educated force to support persistent, networked, and distributed GCC [geographic combatant commander] operations to advance our nation's interests" (R. Thomas, 2017, p. 17).

[2] General Thomas has further noted,

> The value of SOF to their respective geographic combatant commands lies in our global perspective that spans regional boundaries, coupled with our ability to act and influence locally with a range of options; our networked approach that integrates the capabilities of our domestic and international partners, paired with our

Similarly, one former USSOCOM commander observed, "partners, both international and domestic, are critical to providing us with the range of capabilities, resources, and access we require. USSOCOM's extensive investment in building a global network of partners has proven indispensable in developing comprehensive approaches" against threats arising within a complex security environment (Votel, 2016, p. 8). These PND operations are to be optimized and prioritized through the Campaign Plan for Global Special Operations (CP-GSO) and have become a part of SOF doctrine and an underlying—and unifying—concept for the activities that SOF undertake in phases 0 and 1.

PND operations provide a framework for understanding SOF activities to enhance USSOCOM's ability to rapidly respond to, and persistently address, regional contingencies and threats to stability. As JP 3-05 (p. III-2) states,

> All SOF, whether in home station or deployed in support of the GCCs, are part of the global SOF network. Networking allows SOF to exchange information and intelligence and collaborate globally, which is essential to counter transnational and transregional terrorists and other enemies and adversaries. The global SOF network includes nodes and other liaison elements to coordinate and synchronize special operations.

Recent efforts to enable PND operations have focused on the expansion and enhancement of the theater special operations commands (TSOCs) and the completion of USSOCOM's CP-GSO. Starting in 2013, USSOCOM began to increase the number of personnel deployed to its TSOCs, planning an increase of almost 50 percent by 2018. This growth includes significant increases in most staff sections. Additional billets might be approved to provide permanent staffing for special operations commands (SOCs) forward (FWD) within the TSOCs (USSOCOM, undated, 2012; USSOCOM data provided to RAND). By March 2015, some 800 USSOCOM billets had been realigned to the TSOCs in order to increase their capability to provide planning, intelligence, analysis, and communications in support of PND operations (Votel, 2015, p. 15).

A key focus of PND operations is on phase 0 and phase 1 activities designed to shape perceptions, build partners' capabilities, and deter conflict. It is in these "left-of-the-bang" phases that SOF is often optimally deployed as presence, relationships, information, and partner capacity-building are best accomplished prior to a crisis and ideally would prevent threats from emerging in the first place (R. Thomas, 2017,

---

ability to act discreetly against our most important threats; and our seamless integration with the Services to support and enhance their effectiveness, while we provide capabilities that SOF is uniquely structured to deliver. All of these are only possible due to our people—adaptive, agile, flexible, bold, and innovative—who allow us to seize opportunities early, and have strategic impact with a small footprint. (R. Thomas 2016, p. 26) pp. 10–11; Tucker, 2016).[3] Phase 0 (shape) activities are generally designed to "dissuade or deter adversaries and assure friends, as well as set conditions for the contingency plan and are generally conducted through security cooperation activities" (JP 3-0, p. V-8). Phase 1 (deter) activities "deter an adversary from undesirable actions because of friendly capabilities and the will to use them." These activities are "generally weighted toward security activities that are characterized by preparatory actions to protect friendly forces and indicate the intent to execute subsequent phases of the planned operation" (JP 3-0, p. V-8). Phase 0 and phase 1 activities include such things as conducting civil–military operations to mitigate causes of unrest and to build local support for the host nation (HN) among the indigenous population, executing information operations to counter the messaging of extremist organizations, and building the capacity of partner special forces to enable the partner nation (PN) to defeat deter and defeat threats. They also include activities that increase U.S. understanding of the local and regional operating environment and that build relationships that can support current and future operations.

Important elements of PND operations are more-capable TSOCs, greater forward-deployed personnel presence, and enhanced interagency and allied PN partnerships (U.S. Senate, 2016, pp. 25, 27; Votel, 2015; USSOCOM, 2013, pp. ii, 5–6). The TSOC is the primary USSOCOM organization that plans and controls SOF activities within a geographic combatant command. It is tasked with planning and conducting operations in support of the GCC and providing command and control (C2) for attached SOF units. The TSOC, or forward-based elements under its control, is responsible for providing C2 to SOF conducting military engagement, security cooperation (SC), and deterrence operations (JP 3-05, pp. III-4, III-5). As such, the TSOC is the key geographic combatant command–level USSOCOM organization implementing PND operations (JP 3-05, p. III-2). USSOCOM is executing a multiyear process to enhance TSOC capabilities to conduct "full-spectrum" special operations that range from building partner capacity (BPC) to irregular warfare and counterterrorism (McRaven, 2013; USSOCOM, 2013). This expansion includes increasing the number of TSOC personnel and expanding TSOC support functions. These increased capabilities should improve TSOCs' abilities to support PND operations by deepening their regional expertise and improving their capacity for planning, operational oversight, administrative and logistical support, and coordination with other U.S. actors involved in BPC and engagement activities.

---

[3] General Thomas observed in May 2016 that

> left of bang is less a technological approach than a people-access approach: being there ahead of time, having relationships there ahead of time, identifying problems before they become crises, developing that partner capacity, prior, not after, a response. We are too often on the other side of that. (Tucker, 2016)

Greater persistent forward-deployed personnel will occur through the following:

- regionally aligned SOF operational units
- increases in the number of
  - embassy embedded personnel (such as special operations liaison officers [SOLOs] and SOF representatives)
  - TSOC-directed teams executing GCCs' theater campaign plans (such as civil–military support elements [CMSEs], military information support teams [MISTs])
  - SOF liaison elements [SOFLEs])
- increases in
  - persistent rotational security force assistance (through more joint combined exchange training [JCET] and counternarcotic training)
  - SOF exercises
  - forward-deployed C2 elements (SOCs FWD)
  - joint special operations air detachments
  - theater support.

Each of these small teams is discussed in detail in the appendix.

Enhanced interagency partnerships will be fostered through greater information-sharing and coordinated planning in country. Enhanced partnerships with PNs will be built through the International SOF Coordination Center and regional cooperative arrangements to help build effective global SOF partners by improving PN SOF's capacity and interoperability and increasing their ability to collaborate, coordinate, and share information with U.S. SOF.

The Research Question, Approach, and Organization

An important focus of PND operations is phase 0 and phase 1 activities designed to shape perceptions, build partners' capabilities, and deter conflict. Understanding the day-to-day phase 0 and phase 1 operational activities of forward-deployed SOF personnel and the factors that critically influence the outcomes of their tactical operations can help shape USSOCOM efforts to implement PND operations in a manner that better prepares its personnel to support GCC theater campaign plans, work with and leverage critical interagency partners, and strengthen partnerships with like-minded allies. USSOCOM asked RAND to identify key operational challenges that forward-deployed SOF personnel have encountered and to assess whether these operational difficulties can be addressed through PND operations. This analysis can be used to help shape PND operations to better support deployed USSOCOM operators. The bulk of the research for this project was conducted in 2013 and 2014, but the issues and potential solutions identified here remain relevant.[4]

We adopted a multipronged approach to address the main research questions—what are the operational challenges that deployed personnel have encountered, and whether and how PND operations can resolve the operational challenges identified—in which we examined written and oral accounts of SOF personnel's operational experiences in the field during phase 0 and phase 1 missions. As a first step, we examined daily situation reports (SITREPs) and after-action reports (AARs) for SOF personnel deployed throughout U.S. Africa Command (AFRICOM) in 2012 and 2013. We focused on AFRICOM because, increasingly, that geographic combatant command has emerged as an important area of engagement for U.S. SOF, and SOF personnel have undertaken phase 0 and phase 1 missions throughout the region.

One concern that arises by focusing only on SITREPs and AARs from AFRICOM is that the phase 0 and phase 1 operational challenges we identify might be applicable only in AFRICOM. To address this concern, we supplemented our AFRICOM analysis with focus groups for SOF personnel who have been deployed on phase 0 and phase 1 SOF missions globally. Focus-group respondents provided validation that the operational challenges we observed in AFRICOM were broadly applicable in all of the geographic combatant commands to which SOF personnel deployed.

Informed by the results of the analysis of the documents and the findings from the focus groups, we identified key operational challenges that SOF personnel have encountered, and we assessed whether and how PND operations can help mitigate these challenges. We concentrated on security force assistance–oriented missions, typical of phase 0 and phase 1 activities.

This report summarizes our findings. Three key operational challenges stood out across the analyses as having potentially mission-critical adverse consequences.

---

[4]   When this project began, USSOCOM was developing the operational concept of the "global SOF network" (GSN). Building on earlier USSOCOM practice, the GSN envisioned operations based on smaller SOF units working intimately with country-level and local partners to share information and operate effectively and quickly in a complex environment. This entailed integrating two disparate yet jointly important network-building efforts. The first was to build out the technical networks and agreements that would allow units to share information effectively with their partners. These networks for smaller, typically highly trained units were essential to general advances in high-end capabilities worldwide but extended to the integration and interoperation with partners of all types. The second effort was to build out a network that would bring like-minded individuals and organizations that share common interests into communities able to take action (McRaven, 2013; McChrystal, 2011; J. Thomas and Dougherty, 2013). Although the GSN concept is no longer referred to as such in USSOCOM strategy and policy statements, many of its basic principles are contained in the idea of persistent, networked, and distribute operations. In addition, as of mid-2017, the GSN remains embedded in joint doctrine and in the U.S. Army Special Operations Command's operating concept (JP 3-05, 2014; USASOC, 2014). We have reviewed publicly available USSOCOM policy statements and strategy documents published since 2014 and found that, although the terminology might have changed, the emphasis on deploying small teams to persistently and proactively engage with USSOCOM partners remains an important component of USSOCOM's operational approach.

First, SOF personnel often face challenges deconflicting, coordinating, and leveraging SOF activities with those of other U.S. interagency partners. As JP 3-0 highlights, achieving and maintaining unity of effort within and between U.S. forces, the U.S. government, and international partners is a common operating precept. "The synchronization, coordination, and/or integration of military operations with the activities of interorganizational [interagency] partners to achieve unity of effort are key to success, and military forces need to work competently in this environment" (JP 3-0, pp. I-3, III-1). Failure to coordinate effectively with other U.S. interagency partners can lead to mission-critical consequences if SOF personnel lack either the situational awareness or interagency support to carry out their missions or if SOF actions endanger the objectives of their interagency partners.

Second, short SOF deployments with few mechanisms to ensure continuity of effort are an important challenge to building effective, persistent presence and meeting U.S. strategic goals. For phase 0 and phase 1 missions in which SOF personnel build on the work that previously deployed personnel have done, lack of detailed knowledge of past operations and future planned operations can undermine the long-term trajectory and ultimate achievement of GCC objectives.

Third, SOF personnel often found navigating the administrative complexity of contracts, funding procedures, and foreign disclosure and vetting processes challenging. Administrative complexity posed two key problems for SOF personnel. First, it took time away from other tasks that SOF personnel could have been undertaking. For small deployed teams in which each team member is responsible for multiple tasks, increased administrative burdens were seen as a significant erosion of available team capacity. Second, for teams that were unaware of the length of time administrative procedures would take, administrative complexity posed delays that forced teams to revise, truncate, or cancel planned operations.

For most missions, SOF personnel were able to mitigate the operational consequences that poor unity and continuity of effort and administrative complexity posed. However, focus-group respondents emphasized that the time and resource burdens that these operational challenges create, as well as the poor situational awareness they often engender, did pose significant and, at times, mission-critical adverse impacts on mission outcomes.

Of somewhat lesser importance are the challenges noted in relations with PNs and deploying with the right mix of equipment and capabilities; respondents viewed these challenges as less structural or mission critical.

Chapter Two discusses our approach in detail and then summarizes the findings from the analysis of documents and the focus groups. Chapter Three identifies lessons learned for USSOCOM for implementing PND operations.

Identified Operational Challenges

This chapter outlines the details of our approach, followed by a thematically organized set of findings.

Approach

We used a multidimensional approach to identify key operational challenges that SOF personnel have encountered while deployed for phase 0 and phase 1 missions. First, we undertook a document review of daily SITREPs and AARs from AFRICOM. Second, we conducted focus-group sessions with SOF personnel who have been deployed on SOF missions across the geographic combatant commands.

Situation Report Analysis

We examined 117 USSOCOM daily SITREPs from January 2012 to May 2013. SITREPs are daily reports to SOC Africa (SOCAFRICA) that act as a log of units' activities and a mechanism for flagging emerging problems that need to be addressed. As such, SITREPs focus on SOCAFRICA's information requirements. SITREPs are a useful resource for gaining an understanding of SOF activities and noteworthy operational challenges that SOF personnel have encountered while forward deployed. The SITREPs were produced by SOCAFRICA's deputy chief for current operations and collated reporting from SOCAFRICA personnel in Africa. The SITREPs were routed to the joint operations center personnel at AFRICOM.

For each of the 17 months included in the analysis, we read seven consecutive days of SITREPs. We examined a full week of SITREPs from each month to provide a long enough window to track any challenge identified over a multiday window and to understand the context in which it arose. For specific challenges that were not resolved in the seven-day window, we followed their trajectory through additional SITREPs to assess whether there was a resolution to the challenge. We used a random number generator to select the start date. If the selected day would result in a seven-day window that would include days from the following month, we instead selected the last seven days of the month. Figure 2.1 presents the dates for the selected SITREPs.

Figure 2.1
U.S. Africa Command Situation-Report Dates Selected for Analysis

2012

January

S	M	T	W	R	F	S
1	2	3	4	5	**6**	**7**
8	**9**	**10**	**11**	**12**	13	14
15	16	17	18	19	20	21
22	23	24	24	26	27	28
29	30	31				

February

S	M	T	W	R	F	S
			1	2	3	4
5	6	7	8	9	10	11
12	13	14	15	16	17	18
19	20	21	22	**23**	**24**	**25**
26	**27**	**28**	**29**			

March

S	M	T	W	R	F	S
				1	2	3
4	5	6	7	8	9	10
11	12	13	14	15	16	**17**
18	**19**	**20**	**21**	**22**	**23**	24
25	26	27	28	29	30	31

April

S	M	T	W	R	F	S
1	2	3	4	5	6	7
8	9	10	11	12	13	14
15	16	**17**	**18**	**19**	**20**	**21**
22	**23**	24	24	26	27	28
29	30					

May

S	M	T	W	R	F	S
		1	2	3	**4**	**5**
6	**7**	**8**	**9**	**10**	11	12
13	14	15	16	17	18	19
20	21	22	23	24	25	26
27	28	29	30	31		

June

S	M	T	W	R	F	S
					1	2
3	4	**5**	**6**	**7**	**8**	**9**
10	**11**	12	13	14	15	16
17	18	19	20	21	22	23
24	25	26	27	28	29	30

July

S	M	T	W	R	F	S
1	2	3	4	5	6	7
8	9	10	**11**	**12**	**13**	**14**
15	**16**	**17**	18	19	20	21
22	23	24	24	26	27	28
29	30	31				

August

S	M	T	W	R	F	S
			1	2	3	4
5	6	**7**	**8**	**9**	**10**	**11**
12	**13**	14	15	16	17	18
19	20	21	22	23	24	25
26	27	28	29	30	31	

September

S	M	T	W	R	F	S
						1
2	3	4	5	6	**7**	**8**
9	**10**	**11**	**12**	**13**	14	15
16	17	18	19	20	21	22
23	24	25	26	27	28	29
30						

October

S	M	T	W	R	F	S
	1	2	3	4	5	6
7	8	9	10	11	12	13
14	15	16	17	18	19	20
21	22	**23**	**24**	**25**	**26**	**27**
28	**29**	30	31			

November

S	M	T	W	R	F	S
				1	2	3
4	5	6	7	8	**9**	**10**
11	**12**	**13**	**14**	**15**	16	17
18	19	20	21	22	23	24
25	26	27	28	29	30	

December

S	M	T	W	R	F	S
						1
2	3	4	5	6	7	8
9	10	11	12	13	14	15
16	**17**	**18**	**19**	**20**	**21**	**22**
23	24	25	26	27	28	29
30	31					

2013

January

S	M	T	W	R	F	S
		1	2	3	4	5
6	7	8	9	10	11	12
13	14	**15**	**16**	**17**	**18**	**19**
20	**21**	22	23	24	25	26
27	28	29	30	31		

February

S	M	T	W	R	F	S
					1	2
3	4	5	**6**	**7**	**8**	**9**
10	**11**	**12**	13	14	15	16
17	18	19	20	21	22	23
24	25	26	27	28		

March

S	M	T	W	R	F	S
					1	2
3	4	5	6	7	8	**9**
10	**11**	**12**	**13**	**14**	**15**	16
17	18	19	20	21	22	23
24	25	26	27	28	29	30
31						

April

S	M	T	W	R	F	S
	1	2	3	4	5	6
7	8	9	10	11	12	13
14	15	16	**17**	**18**	**19**	**20**
21	**22**	**23**	24	25	26	27
28	29	30				

May

S	M	T	W	R	F	S
			1	2	3	4
5	6	7	8	9	10	**11**
12	13	**14**	**15**	**16**	**17**	**18**
19	20	21	22	23	24	25
26	27	28	29	30		

SOURCE: RAND analysis.
NOTE: There was not a SITREP available for May 13, 2013.
RAND *RR1333-2.1*

It is important to note that SITREPs are not complete records of what SOF personnel were doing on a day-to-day basis. As a result, they often do not provide sufficient insight into why some operational challenges arose or whether the challenges were mission critical, nor do they always include information on the resolution of difficulties encountered. In addition, SITREPs are limited in scope and exclude some important events and activities. Reports on major events were often sent through separate channels. Moreover, some critical SOF assets in Africa—SOLOs are one example—did not report their activities through SITREPs. Examining AARs and discussing challenges with SOF personnel in focus groups address some of the limitations encountered in the SITREP analysis.

After-Action Report Analysis

To gain better insight into how operational challenges might affect mission effectiveness, we examined 71 AFRICOM postmission reports (collectively referred to in this report as AARs) spanning 2009 through 2013. These reports took the form of AARs, special operations debrief and retrieval system reports, and lessons-learned observations. We collected these documents through the USSOCOM Joint Lessons Learned Information System. AARs address some of the shortcomings identified in the SITREP analysis because they reflect SOF personnel assessments at the end of a mission, rather than on a specific day during the mission. As a result, they provide greater insight into the mission criticality of operational challenges and discuss courses of action instigated to address these challenges. Unfortunately, and in contrast to the comprehensiveness of SITREP coverage for SOF activities in AFRICOM, we were limited to a relatively small and nonrandom sample of AARs. Using the 71 AARs, we identified 205 observations about mission challenges that can help inform future PND operations.

Focus Groups

Although mission reporting is a valuable source for identifying challenges that operators have encountered while deployed, they cannot replace direct discussions with SOF personnel. We conducted two focus-group sessions with SOF personnel who were attending the Naval Postgraduate School in Monterey, California, in August 2014. The sample included O-3s, O-4s, and CW-4s from the U.S. Army, Navy, and Air Force, with specialties in civil affairs (CA); psychological operations; special forces; and sea, air, and land teams. Participants' experience reflected deployments in all six geographic combatant commands. In order to protect potentially sensitive or personally identifiable information, we did not collect any information on focus-group participants other than rank, service, and specialty.

We asked focus-group participants to identify mission-critical challenges that they encountered while deployed. Respondents discussed the challenges they faced and contextualized their experiences with regard to the situations (e.g., type of mission and

not having access to office space and motor vehicles to not being allowed in country or being restricted to embassy grounds.

National Security Decision Directive 38 (NSDD 38) gives the COM control over the size and composition of full-time U.S. government personnel in country. U.S. agencies submit NSDD 38 requests to have their personnel included under the COM's mandate for full-time U.S. personnel in country. When an NSDD 38 request is on file for an SOF team, the support that the country team provides to the SOF team is clearly delineated. In many geographic combatant commands, USSOCOM has appeared reluctant to assign personnel formally to the embassies. As a result, for many teams, the relationship between team personnel and the COM is never formalized. Consequently, a situation arises in which embassy support to the SOF teams is provided at COM discretion. The level of embassy support provided might reflect the availability of embassy resources, which are often highly constrained, and whether the COM embraces the SOF team's mission. In many cases, the relationship between the COM and the SOF team is amicable and the embassy can provide support; in other cases, the relationship is more strained and there is less support available for SOF teams. As one focus-group participant noted, "the embassy is very discretionary in their help. If they like you, they'll help you. Otherwise, only if all the NSDD 38 paperwork is in."

The lack of a formal relationship that would be provided through the NSDD 38 process is particularly problematic for SOF teams, such as MIST and CMSE, that depend on embassy resources to complete their missions. Particularly in countries experiencing a surge in U.S. interest, embassy resources are heavily constrained. Because much of the support that embassies provide SOF teams is discretionary, support to SOF might be the first to be cut as embassies find that their resources are not sufficient to meet all of the demands they face. SITREPs, AARs, and focus groups frequently identified lack of embassy office space and accommodations for SOF personnel as an obstacle, and these were a particular problem for MIST and CMSE. As one focus-group participant noted, "Embassy space is hard to come by, and SOF presence is expendable. . . . SOF are temporary faces that can be kicked out at the Ambassador's pleasure."

The informality of the SOF teams' relationship with the country team also raises the issue of authorities when SOF teams receive conflicting guidance from the TSOC and the embassy. For one focus-group participant, differences between the TSOC and the embassy impeded the team's ability to carry out its mission. He found that "verbal agreements [between the TSOC and embassy] fall apart and become authorities questions."

SOF disagreements with country teams about constraints under which SOF teams operate in country exacerbate the personality-based overtones to SOF–country team relationships. The COM has authority over such issues as the number of U.S. personnel in country, force protection requirements, and interactions with HN personnel. All three have been contentious issues between SOF teams and embassy staff. Of the three, force caps have been the most common and reflect distinct differences in environmental assessments by State Department and SOF personnel. As one focus-group participant noted, "we had issues about the number of people on the ground. The SOCFWD wanted more capability, but the Ambassador said no and had strict level limits." Another participant followed up and argued that "the force cap is built on the ambassador's perception, not partner nation demand. So, the ambassador is afraid of another [operational detachment—alpha] in country, but the partner nation is banging down our door for more." These comments highlight the different perspectives the COM and SOF personnel can have on national policy and HN security issues.

Overall, SOF teams' mission effectiveness appears greater when there is transparency and trust in teams' interactions with the embassy country team. Our SITREP analysis followed a case in which the eroding relationship and lack of transparency between a SOFLE in an African country and the country's COM reduced the support and trust that teams received from the embassy.

Low Integration Between Special Operations Forces Teams

Although most of the unity-of-effort challenges discussed in the SITREPs, AARs, and focus groups revolved around SOF–State Department relations, intra-SOF unity-of-effort concerns arose as well. One focus-group participant highlighted that having competing chains of command, as well as lack of insight into other SOF activities in country, has resulted in missed opportunities for synergies across U.S. efforts. He found that "[SOF] people deployed in country may all be operating under different orders, with different chains of command and effort." For example, he was involved in a JCET that included a visit to a refugee camp. He and his team thought that including a CA team that was already in country on the visit would have been helpful to them and to the CA team. However, he and his team decided that they did not have the authority to include the CA team.

Continuity of Effort

Most SOF teams deploy for relatively short periods of time. Deployments could be as short as a few weeks or extend to six to nine months. With the exception of such positions as SOLOs, SOF deployments rarely extend to one year. SOF personnel identified short deployments with very few mechanisms to ensure continuity of effort as an important challenge to building effective, persistent presence and meeting U.S. strategic objectives. For phase 0 and phase 1 missions in which SOF personnel build on the work that previously deployed personnel have done, lack of detailed knowledge of past operations and future planned operations can undermine the long-term trajectory and ultimate achievement of GCC objectives. This concern was notable in SITREPs, AARs, and the focus groups.

SOF personnel viewed short deployment durations for liaison positions (i.e., SOFLEs and liaison officers) as especially challenging given the need for liaisons to build personal relationships and the importance of the liaison for supporting other SOF activities in country. Moreover, SOF personnel reported that they received frequent criticism from embassy country teams because of their short deployments. SITREPs highlighted country teams' concerns about the relatively short deployments of SOF temporary-duty personnel and suggested that SOFLE and other enduring SOF engagement elements be deployed on a permanent-change-of-station basis for a longer period of time. Liaison duties embedded within operational teams exacerbated the challenges associated with short deployment liaison positions because it is difficult for operational team members to maintain their team duties as well as liaison duties.

Beyond the importance of continuity in liaison elements, MISTs also identified lack of continuity as a key challenge for meeting their strategic objectives. MISTs work on information instruments that span multiple deployments. Short-duration deployments coupled with poor to nonexistent documentation for subsequent teams have resulted in dropped products and degraded teams' ability to build on past efforts. Multiple MISTs noted the importance of having longer-deployed (e.g., permanent change of station) military information support operations (MISO) personnel at SOCAFRICA global operations to support the continuity of operations between temporary-duty MISTs.

Administrative Complexity

SOF personnel often found navigating the administrative complexity of contracts, funding procedures, and foreign disclosure and vetting processes challenging. Administrative complexity posed two key problems for SOF personnel. First, it took time away from other tasks that SOF personnel could have been undertaking. For small deployed teams in which each team member is responsible for multiple tasks, respondents saw increased administrative burdens as a significant erosion of available team capacity. Second, for teams that were unaware of the length of time administrative procedures would take, administrative complexity posed delays that forced teams to revise, truncate, or cancel planned operations.

Contracting Constraints

Although SOF personnel negotiate contracts for many goods and services while deployed, the most challenging mission-critical contract appears to be for hiring interpreters. The difficulty in securing the services of good interpreters was discussed throughout the SITREPs, AARs, and focus groups. Interpreters who can work effectively with SOF units are difficult to find, particularly in areas using languages with small populations of users. Without competent interpreters, special operators can neither collect nor impart information effectively.

SOF interpreters must be fluent in English and the local dialect and proficient in both languages in the technical terms used to explain and carry out the mission tasks. They must be able to get clearance and physically capable of working with SOF and PN personnel. The administrative processes that make it difficult to write a sole-source contract or put an interpreter "on retainer" further complicate hiring an effective interpreter.

Focus-group participants voiced many frustrations about the difficulties in finding and retaining effective interpreters. Taken together, participants uniformly identified one key change made to the procedures under which they hire interpreters: the ability to hire a reliable, specialized interpreter through a sole-source contract. A sole-source contracting process would allow SOF teams to hire an interpreter without providing for full and open competition for the position.

Focus-group participants offered two main reasons for wanting a sole-sourcing capability for hiring interpreters. First, once the right interpreter has been found, they do not want to lose that candidate. Second, SOF personnel do not want to reveal their operations by advertising for contractors.[2]

Funding Approval and Disbursement Procedures

Many teams noted difficulties in navigating the funding process, particularly when the funding process differed from the one in which the team's contracting or paying agent was trained. A Marine Special Operations Team on a JCET laid out a representative example of some of the challenges that teams have encountered. It found that, although the team had deployed with a field ordering officer and paying agent who had completed their certifications, the procedures for which they had been trained differed from those in place for the JCET. As a result, the team had been unable to close its accounts locally and had to reach back to the Camp Lejeune contracting office to clear the accounts.

Other teams noted that delays in receiving funding approval have led to the cancellation of SOF activities. As one focus-group participant discussed, "we miss programs because of funding and contracting issues." MISO activities appear particularly vulnerable to funding delays.[3]

Foreign Disclosure and Vetting Processes

Many teams found that the foreign disclosure and vetting processes for foreign personnel took longer than the team had expected because of delays on either the U.S. or HN part. Incomplete vetting has resulted in truncated or canceled training missions.

---

[2]   More broadly, some focus-group participants were concerned that their need to hold open bidding processes for other contracts created potential operational security concerns.

[3]   Our analysis focused on the funding concerns facing deployed teams. As the TSOCs are expanded, they could face increased issues of funding complexity as well because they are responsible for the design of a greater number of programs that are funded through an array of funding authorities.

Other Challenges

In addition to key unity- and continuity-of-effort and administrative complexity challenges, SOF personnel also encountered challenges in PN interactions and in deploying with the right mix of equipment and capabilities.

Partner-Nation Interactions
Information-Sharing with Partner Countries

Although information-sharing with partners was not a challenge commonly included in SITREPs and AARs, focus-group participants identified it as a particularly thorny problem that many had encountered. Issues over information-sharing frequently eroded PN personnel's trust in U.S. SOF personnel; even in situations in which personnel could maintain trust, it reduced the attractiveness of working with the United States.

One participant identified what he perceived as a particularly egregious example of the asymmetries in the information that SOF personnel receive from their partners versus what SOF personnel could share. He had received photographic intelligence from one of the PN officers with whom he had been working and had been asked by the PN officer to use U.S. resources to clean up the image quality. He did so, and, when the PN officer received the cleaned-up image, access to it had been restricted to a level that the PN officer no longer had clearance to view. The new image that the focus-group participant could share with the PN officer was of worse quality than the original image. As a result of this incident, the U.S. officer's credibility with the PN officer eroded and adversely affected his relationship with the PN personnel.

More generally, participants emphasized throughout the focus groups that relationships with PN personnel are personality driven and are based on trust and credibility. They identified constraints on their ability to share information with PN personnel as an important concern for maintaining trust in SOF personnel and demonstrating SOF credibility. As one participant remarked on PN personnel's perceptions of the benefits of working with SOF with regard to constraints on sharing information and on deploying with PN personnel, "Our partners ask us 'what use is the United States?' In their eyes, we can't deploy, we can train, but we can't share. What are we bringing to the fight?" Other focus-group participants echoed this perception of frustration on the part of PN personnel. One respondent sympathized with the challenges other operators had faced with regard to constraints on information-sharing but pointed out that, although operators often feel that they ought to be allowed to release information to their partners, USSOCOM does not control or restrict the intelligence it receives. He argued that USSOCOM needs to do a better job educating operators on when and how intelligence can be shared.

Recognizing the limits on information-sharing at the outset of a mission could help structure SOF interactions with PN and forestall erosion in trust.

Partner-Nation Personnel and Equipment Shortfalls

Most training missions focus on training complete, existing PN units (e.g., a platoon or company) for an entire course of instruction. Training has often been degraded either because the whole unit is not available for training or because individuals are not available for the entire training period. Similarly, SOF teams have experienced degraded training activities when working with partner units stood up solely for the training.

For training missions, many teams plan on using equipment supplied by the PN. For many deployments, the equipment that partner countries have promised to supply is available and sufficient for the mission. In some cases, however, the PN equipment is either unavailable or unsuitable for use in the training mission. In these cases, equipment shortfalls have led to bottlenecks and degraded mission performance.

Deploying with the Right Mix of Equipment and Capabilities

The two most common challenges facing deployed teams with regard to team members' skill sets and their equipment were (1) the language capabilities and cultural expertise and (2) communication equipment. For teams working in the human domain, lack of low-visibility body armor was also mentioned.

Team Language and Culture Skills

A common thread running through the documentation from and discussions with SOF personnel operating in the human domain was teams' lack of language or appropriate regional and cultural knowledge capabilities. Several teams believed that the lack of appropriate language skills was detrimental to mission execution. As described above, administrative challenges that made hiring effective interpreters difficult exacerbated this problem. As one team working in a part of French-speaking Africa experienced, although the team was strong on tactical qualifications, only one member of the team spoke any French. This made it very difficult for the team to work effectively with PN forces or the local population.

Equipment Shortfalls

Most teams appeared well-equipped to carry out their missions. For teams that did note equipment challenges in their mission documentation, communication equipment and low-visibility armor were the two areas in which equipment shortfalls might have been mission critical.

The most common U.S. equipment shortfall noted in the SITREPs and AARs was communication equipment. As one focus-group participant commented succinctly, "restricted access to communications is problematic." Concerns focused on teams' ability to communicate with each other, with headquarters elements, and with HN personnel. To communicate within a team while deployed, team members rely on access to mobile satellite and cellular equipment. In particular, teams have emphasized the importance of international cell phones to augment their communication options.

For reachback to headquarters, teams identified two constraints. First, access to and maintenance of secure communication channels is challenging. Second, even for teams with access to secure communications, many have had difficulty accessing particular domains in which mission-relevant information is stored. These difficulties can stem from restricted access to the specific portals or, for longer-deployed teams, the expiration of encryption keys.

In cases in which U.S. and HN communication systems are not interoperable, SOF teams' ability to communicate with partner units is low.

The second most common equipment shortfall that teams mentioned was low-visibility body armor. In particular, teams recommended that SOF personnel who need to wear civilian attire while interacting with locals ought to be issued low-visibility body armor. They believed that wearing body armor on key-leader engagements would be seen as a sign of distrust, and, as a result, some teams chose not to wear visible body armor.

CHAPTER THREE

Implications for Persistent, Networked, and Distributed Special Operations

Our analyses identified three main operational challenges. First, SOF personnel often face challenges deconflicting, coordinating, and leveraging SOF activities with those of other U.S. interagency partners (i.e., unity of effort). Second, short SOF deployments with few mechanisms to ensure continuity of effort are an important challenge to building effective, persistent presence and meeting U.S. strategic goals (i.e., continuity of effort). Third, SOF personnel often found navigating the administrative complexity of contracts, funding procedures, and foreign disclosure and vetting processes challenging (i.e., administrative complexity). Although SOF personnel were often able to mitigate the adverse operational consequences that poor unity and continuity of effort and administrative complexity posed, the time and resource burdens that these operational challenges create, as well as the poor situational awareness they engender, risk degrading teams' effectiveness in current and future missions. In this chapter, we address the question, "Can USSOCOM mitigate these challenges through the key elements of PND operations?"

During the focus groups, we asked participants for their thoughts on whether and how USSOCOM could address these challenges through PND operations. Important elements of PND operations are (1) more-capable TSOCs, (2) greater forward-deployed personnel presence, and (3) enhanced interagency and allied PN partnerships.

Focus-group participants' reactions were mixed. Although many participants felt that each of these elements could be used to mitigate the challenges they had experienced, they believed that success would depend crucially on how PND operations were implemented. This was especially true with regard to staffing enhanced TSOCs. Focus-group participants' reactions highlighted the importance of implementation for success, their relative unfamiliarity with the PND concept, and the opportunity for outreach to operators about the operational benefits of PND operations.

Enhanced Theater Special Operations Commands

One of the purposes of PND operations is to regularize a USSOCOM theater-level presence that parallels many of the theater SC roles and missions currently planned and executed by the Department of State and GCCs. Enhanced TSOCs could provide a good mechanism for increasing unity and continuity of effort, as well as streamlining some of the administrative tasks that currently deployed personnel perform. Focus-group participants were most concerned that the benefits of enhanced TSOCs would depend crucially on staffing decisions for TSOC personnel. Participants saw personnel with both USSOCOM- and geographic combatant command–specific backgrounds as the most valuable additions to the TSOCs.

Increasing the size of the TSOCs should improve their ability to support the PND operations by deepening their regional expertise and improving their capacity for planning, operational oversight, administrative and logistical support, and coordination with other U.S. actors involved in BPC and engagement activities. The improved capacity for planning and operational oversight could help ensure that engagement activities were coordinated with the interagency, built on previous engagement with the PN, and continued across the deployments of rotating SOF units. The enlarged TSOCs would also have a greater capacity to support deployed SOF personnel administratively by filling their financial and contractual support requirements. Finally, greater TSOC involvement in engagement activity could help overcome some of the problems inherent in the relatively short deployments of the SOF elements executing engagement activities.

Focus-group participants had mixed reactions when asked whether enhanced TSOCs would mitigate operational challenges. In part, their reactions reflected incomplete information about what tasks enhanced TSOCs would take on and where the increased personnel would come from. There was strong support for increasing the contracting capabilities embedded in TSOCs. As one participant argued,

> we need a contracting officer at least at the TSOC; someone in theater, who can distribute cash. We had to have someone on the team leave Africa to go to Italy to take care of this. The whole process took 30 days, and had to be done every three months.

Participants also saw enhanced contracting capabilities at the TSOC as a potential solution to difficulties in hiring interpreters. One participant speculated that "perhaps GSN can streamline the process. GSN may provide a mechanism to identify qualified and effective interpreters, and develop a contract vehicle. This may be most possible for persistent routine activities such as annual exercises."[1]

Other participants argued that, instead of staffing an enhanced TSOC to address administrative requirements, they would prefer to see more support to address interagency and HN relationships. As one participant suggested, "push manpower down to the embassy rather than the theater."

---

[1]   During the time period when we conducted this research (2013–2014), the term *global SOF network* (GSN) was used to describe PND operations.

How successfully TSOCs will mitigate operational challenges could depend on how enhanced TSOCs are staffed. Focus-group participants were concerned about the SOF- and geographic combatant command–specific expertise of TSOC staff. The majority of focus-group participants supported the claim that USSOCOM "needs to populate the TSOC with people from that theater." They believed that, if personnel came from outside of the SOF community and had no familiarity with the theater, they would not understand SOF-specific needs.

Conversely, for situations in which positions were staffed from within the SOF community, SOF focus-group participants were concerned about where the staff would come from and how suitable the personnel would be for the billets. Focus-group participants viewed TSOC billets, as well as forward-deployed liaison positions, such as SOFLE and SOC FWD, as detrimental for career progress. As one participant asked, "is there going to be an expansion of billets? Right now there is a perception these billets are career killers. This needs to be changed. Make it a priority so guys don't get smashed career wise."

Greater Forward-Deployed Personnel Presence

Increasing the number of units and personnel deployed in theater could exacerbate unity- and continuity-of-effort challenges but could also provide mechanisms for increasing unity and continuity of effort to achieve U.S. strategic objectives.

Enhanced Role for Liaison Elements

Focus-group participants identified SOFLEs, such as SOLOs and other liaison officers, as linchpins for improving unity and continuity of effort. Increasing SOFLEs and extending their deployments could strengthen key nodes required for PND operations, but only if liaisons have the time to build the requisite personal relations and resources to support other SOF activities in country. One participant commented that "length of deployment matters. There is a very transient approach to SOF in embassy; eight- or nine-month chunks are too short. We can't develop relationships. Make deployments [for liaisons] one year minimum." This argument was echoed throughout the SITREPs and AARs, with one liaison officer also highlighting the steep learning curve that liaison officers experience.

In addition to the length of liaison elements' deployments, focus-group participants emphasized the need for the "right" personnel for these billets. Participants argued that liaisons should be mature, generally stipulating that an O-4 or O-5 would be the right rank.[2] Liaisons should have requisite language and cultural skills. The key challenge participants saw for enhancing liaison elements was that these positions

---

[2] Mission documentation echoed this preference.

pulled SOF personnel away from group positions and were seen as detrimental for career progress.

Staggered Deployments for Key Personnel

In addition to longer deployments for liaison elements, increasing deployments for operational teams was also a common recommendation in the AARs and SITREPs. This might be less critical if key liaison elements were deployed for longer periods of time and could manage both unity and continuity of effort.

In the absence of longer deployments for nonliaison elements, many reports identified staggered deployments as a mechanism to increase continuity of effort. Some teams have used staggered deployment schedules successfully to increase continuity of effort. For Horn of Africa MISO teams, respondents saw 90-day offset deployment schedules for regional information support teams and MISTs as a safeguard for continuity of effort.

Enhanced Interagency and Allied Partner-Nation Partnerships

In order to prevent duplication of effort, uncoordinated activities, or conflicting efforts, it is important that PND operations be well coordinated with both the COMs and the GCCs. Coordination with the COM is particularly important because the COM must approve all activities occurring within his or her country. Three main lines of effort were highlighted for enhancing interagency partnerships: (1) use the NSDD 38 process to formalize relations with COMs; (2) include SOF and GCC planning within broader U.S. strategic planning at the country level, preferably through the mission strategic resource planning process; and (3) educate SOF and the interagency about their respective activities, capabilities, and responsibilities. All three lines of effort go beyond solutions that USSOCOM can address independently through its implementation of PND operations. Using the NSDD 38 process to formalize relations with COMs might be the most straightforward to set in place because the NSDD 38 process already exists.

One of the focuses of PND operations is the building of relationships. Enhanced relations with PNs might be built through greater forward-deployed presence. Regional and international coordination centers can provide additional venues to build relationships, share information, and increase interoperability.

Focus-group respondents were supportive of mechanisms that would strengthen their abilities to build personal relationships with PN personnel and access more information about personnel. A few participants noted that they would like to see the International SOF Coordination Center track information about HN personnel and provide an accessible database from which operators could identify PN personnel to approach and find out details about the person's background. As one participant noted, "it is frustrating to find out the partner nation commander was in a lot of U.S.

programs, and there is *no* record of what he did." Cultivating an improved understanding within USSOCOM of the information available within the SC community could help address this problem because the in-country SC office and DATT and the Defense Security Cooperation Agency are responsible for tracking PN personnel who have received U.S. training and education. In addition, one recent USSOCOM effort to mitigate this problem is the development of the global SOF common operational picture. The global SOF common operational picture will serve as a common data set on information about partner SOF (see Eaton et al., 2014).

One lesson that emerged from the focus groups is the need to ensure that PNs also benefit from PND operations. If the network components are seen as solely for the benefit of the United States, they might foster resentment rather than cooperation. One concrete example of this emerged in a conversation about the benefits of the battlefield information collection and exploitation system as a platform for better information-sharing. Although battlefield information collection and exploitation system terminals were provided for large joint missions, because they were going to be removed when the United States left, they were not seen as a mechanism for fostering cooperation. If the United States had planned to leave them in place and use them for continued information-sharing with its partners, they might have served as a source of goodwill. Instead, focus-group participants believed, they were a source of resentment.

Final Observations

Implementing three of the main PND operation elements—(1) more-capable TSOCs, (2) greater forward-deployed personnel presence, and (3) enhanced interagency and allied PN partnerships—can provide USSOCOM opportunities to address the three key operational challenges that forward-deployed SOF personnel experienced during phase 0 and phase 1 missions: unity of effort, continuity of effort, and administrative complexity. However, these opportunities will depend crucially on how the PND operations are implemented. Figure 3.1 presents our assessment of whether each key element of PND operations is capable of addressing the three main operational challenges facing SOF teams and identifies the instruments available, if any, within the PND operational element to address each operational challenge.

As a critical element of PND operations, enhanced TSOCs have the potential to improve greatly SOF effectiveness and provide the greatest leverage to address the operational challenges identified in this report. Enhanced TSOCs will have greater capacity to provide administrative support to forward-deployed teams, coordinate SOF activities across teams and across deployments, and play a greater role in GCC activity planning and maintaining communications with embassy teams. Of all of the potential mitigation strategies that PND operations might provide, enhanced administrative support to deployed teams is most directly related to current and projected TSOC

Figure 3.1
Persistent, Networked, and Distributed Special Operations Elements Could Mitigate Key Operational Challenges

		Operational challenges		
		Unity of effort	**Continuity of effort**	**Administrative complexity**
Enhanced TSOCs	*Capable of addressing challenge?*	Maybe	Yes	Yes
	Instruments	• Increased planning with GCC • Increased communication with embassy country teams	• Coordinate SOF activities across deployments	• Enhanced administrative support to deployed teams
Increased forward deployments	*Capable of addressing challenge?*	Maybe	Yes	No
	Instruments	• Increase situational awareness of other U.S. efforts in theater • Ensure that SOF activities are coordinated with other U.S. efforts	• Provide more teams over time • Ensure that successive teams are well-briefed on previous activities	
Enhanced interagency and allied partnerships	*Capable of addressing challenge?*	Maybe	Maybe	No
	Instruments	• Increased whole-of-government planning process • Increased planning with PNs	• Increased whole-of-government planning process • Increased planning with PNs	

PND elements

SOURCE: RAND analysis.

RAND RR1333-3.1

activities and is most likely to occur. However, although enhanced TSOCs might be well-placed organizations to address SOF personnel's concerns about unity and continuity of effort, without taking these challenges into account when implementing enhanced TSOCs, these improvements could be less likely to occur.

Some improvements accruing to enhanced TSOCs will stem directly from the higher personnel numbers assigned to it and the consequent removal of constraints on its ability to engage in the full range of planning and coordination activities. But according to the SOF personnel who took part in our focus groups, the assignment of appropriately trained staff to the TSOCs for extended periods of time is essential in order to ensure that all the gains of more-robust TSOCs are realized. By *appropriately trained*, we are referring to personnel with a deep understanding of SOF operations and regional knowledge of the area of operations. To ensure continuity, these personnel also need to remain in their posts for extended periods of time because there is no substitute for relationship-building with GCCs, embassies, and PNs. *In short, robust TSOCs are not just about more numbers but also about high-quality personnel.*

USSOCOM's ability to address unity-of-effort concerns through enhanced TSOCs will depend crucially on what other steps USSOCOM takes to enhance interagency partnerships. For example, if USSOCOM continues to deploy SOF teams outside the NSDD 38 process, and if GCC theater campaign planning and State Department mission strategic resource planning processes are uncoordinated, enhanced TSOCs will be hampered in their ability to increase effective communication between SOF teams and the COM.

Increased forward deployments also have the potential to enhance the impact of SOF activities. The most direct contribution of increased forward deployments will be greater unity of effort in which teams can ensure that their successors are well-briefed on previous activities. This effect can be enhanced if the activities are coordinated with other interagency efforts and build on prior SOF activities with partner forces. That implies good planning, information-sharing, and visibility into the activities that the services conduct and monitoring of progress toward clearly established goals. A similarly well-coordinated set of planning processes with partners can enhance the value of SOF activities. *These benefits, however, might be contingent upon the length of deployment, a deeper understanding of the interagency by USSOCOM personnel, and improved predeployment preparation.*

Enhanced interagency and allied partnerships are a key element in USSOCOM's strategies for future operations. Without stronger interagency and allied partnerships, it will be difficult for USSOCOM to address the unity-of-effort challenges that its operators have faced. Better whole-of-government planning processes and more-formal relationships between SOF teams and the COM will forestall some of the operational challenges that operators have encountered. However, given the constraints under which COMs operate, these challenges are unlikely to disappear entirely.

PND operations highlight the importance of building networks within SOF, throughout U.S. interagency organizations, and with PNs. The networked structure supporting these operations is designed to increase situational awareness and increase USSOCOM's ability to contribute to cooperative efforts to mitigate regional challenges and accomplish GCCs' theater campaign plans. Importantly, the most common operational challenges that forward-deployed SOF personnel have encountered are issues of situational awareness and leveraging SOF activities to accomplish theater objectives. As such, PND operations provide a good framework for addressing the key operational challenges that forward-deployed SOF personnel experience. To maximize PND operations' ability to address these challenges, they need to be taken into account as they are implemented.

Persistent-Presence Special Operations Forces Small Teams

Civil Military Support Element

A CMSE is a task-organized CA unit rotationally deployed to an HN to support the TSOC's civil–military engagement (CME) plan. CME activities are intended to support U.S. global counterterrorism efforts against violent extremist organizations and are coordinated with the GCC's phase 0 theater campaign plan and synchronized with relevant the State Department's country strategies. The CMSEs plan, prepare, execute, and assess CME activities. The CMSE provides direct support to the U.S. embassy and can provide general support to other SOF organizations deployed to the HN. A CMSE is generally built around a four-soldier CA team from a U.S. Army SOC regionally aligned CA battalion to which a two-soldier planning element has been added. Other CA enablers can supplement it as necessary (JP 3-05, p. II-18; JP 3-57, p. II-6; Field Manual 3-57, pp. 3-27–3-28, GL-6).

Counternarcoterrorism

Counternarcoterrorism activities provide counternarcotics assistance and training for foreign security forces. Counternarcoterrorism missions are executed in support of a GCC's theater campaign plan and are intended both to provide USSOCOM unit training and to increase the PN's capacity to engage and defeat narcoterrorism within its borders (U.S. Air Force SOC Instruction 10-204, pp. 4, 17; Brown, 2010, pp. 3, 24, 49).

Joint Combined Exchange Training

JCET is a training program conducted overseas to fulfill U.S. forces' training requirements and to exchange the sharing of skills between U.S. forces and their HN counterparts (JP 3-05, p. GL-8). JCETs are primarily executed by operational detachments—alpha or sea, air, and land platoons.

Joint Special Operations Aviation Detachment

A joint special operations aviation detachment (JSOAD) is a scalable, tactical-level C2 organization. A JSOAD is deployed when mission requirements or the operating environment necessitates a geographically separated force with an intermediate C2 node to achieve mission. The JSOAD is responsible for tactical planning and force generation to accomplish the missions assigned to it (Air Force Instruction 10-410, p. 22). The mission aircraft assigned to a JSOAD are often owned, operated, and maintained by contractors.

Military Information Support Team

A MIST is a task-organized active-component MISO element rotationally deployed to an HN to perform persistent, population-centric engagement in support of the GCC and COM. It plans, coordinates, and executes MISO in support of GCC, TSOC, and COM tactical- and operation-level objectives (USSOCOM, 2014).

Special Operations Command Forward

An SOC FWD is a tailored, operational-level headquarters element that provides forward-deployed persistence presence and C2 in a theater of operations. The SOC FWD has a close working relationship with the associated country team and HN forces (JP 3-05, p. III-5).

Special Operations Force Liaison Element

A SOFLE is a task-organized rotational SOF element consisting of one or more experienced SOF officers or senior enlisted personnel deployed to a specific HN or embedded within a coalition force to conduct liaison activities. The SOFLE coordinates, assesses, and recommends training, equipping, and engagement opportunities with the HN force or provides the connectivity and synchronization of expeditionary forces. A TSOC can establish a SOFLE on a temporary basis in countries that do not have a SOLO or SOF representative in order to directly support SC goals and objectives. SOFLEs are attached to the U.S. embassy, PN forces, or coalition forces and coordinate with HN forces (JP 3-05, p. III-22).

Special Operations Forces Representative

An SOF representative is an experienced SOF officer proficient in the language of the HN who is assigned to the country team in select countries. The SOF representative is under COM authority and serves as the primary adviser to the SDO/DATT, the country team, and the HN's SOF leadership. SOF representatives are operationally and tactically focused and coordinate efforts to develop the tactical capabilities of HN SOF units. The SOF representative coordinates tactical- and operational-level SOF activities (local theater and global) in support of the COM; commander of TSOC; GCC; and U.S. and HN SOC equities. The SOF representative also maintains visibility on all U.S. SOF activities inside an HN and coordinates those activities with the SDO/DATT (JP 3-05, pp. xiii, III-22).

Special Operations Liaison Officer

A SOLO is an experienced SOF officer with language, cultural, military, and civilian training, in addition to SOF staff experience. A SOLO is generally assigned to the HN's national SOF headquarters as part of an enduring SOF presence in select countries. The SOLO operates under COM authority and is the commander of USSOCOM's direct representative and the primary SOF adviser to the SDO/DATT, the country team, and the HN's SOF leadership. The SOLO focuses on developing and maintaining the HN's SOF command and its institutional relationships with other HN government ministries. The SOLO also monitors all SOF activities in the HN and coordinates in-country, theater, and global SOF activities in support of the COM, the commander of TSOC, GCC, and U.S. and HN SOC equities at the strategic level (JP 3-05, pp. xiii, III-20–III-21).

References

Air Force Instruction 10-410—*See* Secretary of the Air Force, 2015.

Brown, Phillip B., *USSOCOM's Role in Addressing Human Trafficking*, Fort Leavenworth, Kan.: School of Advanced Military Studies, U.S. Army Command and General Staff College, 2010. As of December 10, 2015:
https://www.hsdl.org/?view&did=717569

Commander, U.S. Air Force Special Operations Command, *AFSOC Joint Exercise Program (JEP)*, Air Force Special Operations Command Instruction 10-204, December 18, 2014. As of December 10, 2015:
http://static.e-publishing.af.mil/production/1/afsoc/publication/afsoci10-204/afsoci10-204.pdf

Defense Institute of Security Assistance Management, *The Management of Security Cooperation*, 32nd ed., January 2013.

Eaton, Derek, Angela O'Mahony, Walter Nelson, Jeremy Boback, Jonathan P. Wong, Thomas S. Szayna, and William Welser IV, *The Global Special Operations Forces Common Operating Picture Database*, Santa Monica, Calif.: RAND Corporation, 2014. Not available to the general public.

Field Manual 3-57—*See* Headquarters, Department of the Army, 2011.

Headquarters, Department of the Army, *Civil Affairs Operations*, Washington, D.C., Field Manual 3-57, October 2011. As of December 10, 2015:
http://armypubs.army.mil/doctrine/DR_pubs/dr_a/pdf/fm3_57.pdf

JP 3-0—*See* U.S. Joint Chiefs of Staff, 2011.

JP 3-05—*See* U.S. Joint Chiefs of Staff, 2014.

JP 3-57—*See* U.S. Joint Chiefs of Staff, 2013.

McChrystal, Stanley A., "It Takes a Network: The New Front Line of Modern Warfare," *Foreign Policy*, February 21, 2011. As of December 10, 2015:
http://foreignpolicy.com/2011/02/21/it-takes-a-network/

McRaven, William H., *Posture Statement of Admiral William H. McRaven, USN Commander, United States Special Operations Command, Before the 113th Congress House Armed Services Committee*, Washington, D.C.: U.S. House of Representatives, March 6, 2013. As of December 9, 2015:
http://docs.house.gov/meetings/AS/AS00/20130306/100394/HHRG-113-AS00-Wstate-McRavenUSNA-20130306.pdf

Miles, Donna, "Socom Officials Work on Plan for Global Network," *DoD News*, June 3, 2013. As of December 9, 2015:
http://archive.defense.gov/news/newsarticle.aspx?id=120193

NSDD 38—*See* U.S. Department of State, 1982.

Secretary of the Air Force, *Operations Planning: Presentation of Air Force Special Operations Forces*, Air Force Instruction 10-410, January 7, 2010, certified current February 28, 2012.

Thomas, Jim, and Christopher Dougherty, *Beyond the Ramparts: The Future of U.S. Special Operations Forces*, Washington, D.C.: Center for Strategic and Budgetary Assessments, May 10, 2013. As of December 10, 2015:
http://csbaonline.org/publications/2013/05/
beyond-the-ramparts-the-future-of-u-s-special-operations-forces/

Thomas, Raymond A., III, "Prologue," *Prism: Special Operations in a Chaotic World*, Vol. 6, No. 3, 2016, pp. 2–3. As of June 21, 2017:
http://cco.ndu.edu/Portals/96/Documents/prism/prism_6-3/
Prism%20Vol%206%20No%203a.pdf?ver=2016-12-09-115330-500

———, U.S. Army, commander, U.S. Special Operations Command, statement before the U.S. Senate Committee on Armed Services, May 4, 2017. As of June 21, 2017:
https://www.armed-services.senate.gov/imo/media/doc/Thomas_05-04-17.pdf

Tucker, Patrick, "America's New Special Operations Commander Wants to Predict the Future," *Defense One*, May 25, 2016. As of June 21, 2017:
http://www.defenseone.com/threats/2016/05/
americas-new-special-operations-commander-wants-predict-future/128583/

U.S. Air Force SOC Instruction 10-204—*See* Commander, U.S. Air Force Special Operations Command, 2014.

U.S. Army Special Operations Command, *ARSOF Operating Concept 2022*, September 26, 2014. As of June 21, 2017:
http://www.soc.mil/Assorted%20Pages/ARSOF%20Operating%20Concept%202014.pdf

U.S. Department of State, "Staffing at Diplomatic Missions and Their Overseas Constituent Posts," National Security Decision Directive 38, June 2, 1982. As of December 10, 2015:
http://www.state.gov/m/pri/nsdd/45148.htm

U.S. Joint Chiefs of Staff, *Joint Operations*, Washington, D.C., Joint Publication 3-0, August 11, 2011. As of December 9, 2015:
http://purl.fdlp.gov/GPO/gpo30082

———, *Civil–Military Operations*, Washington, D.C., Joint Publication 3-57, September 11, 2013. As of December 10, 2015:
http://www.dtic.mil/doctrine/new_pubs/jp3_57.pdf

———, *Special Operations*, Washington, D.C., Joint Publication 3-05, July 16, 2014. As of December 9, 2015:
http://www.dtic.mil/doctrine/new_pubs/jp3_05.pdf

U.S. Senate, Committee on Armed Services, *Advance Policy Questions for Lieutenant General Raymond A. Thomas, USA, Nominee for Commander, United States Special Operations Command*, Washington, D.C., March 9, 2016. As of June 21, 2017:
https://www.armed-services.senate.gov/imo/media/doc/Thomas_03-09-16.pdf

USSOCOM—*See* U.S. Special Operations Command.

U.S. Special Operations Command, *TSOC Quick Wins*, undated.

———, *Special Operations Command ROC Drill 3: TSOC HQs Base-Lining*, October 18, 2012.

———, *SOCOM 2020: Forging the Tip of the Spear*, c. 2013. As of December 9, 2015:
http://www.defenseinnovationmarketplace.mil/resources/SOCOM2020Strategy.pdf

————, *US Special Operation Command Implementation Guidance for Global Campaign Plan— Special Operations 7000-14 (USSOCOM IG GCP-SO)*, draft version 6.0, April 2014. Not available to the general public.

————, *2017 Fact Book*, c. 2016. As of March 15, 2017:
http://www.socom.mil/FactBook/2017%20Fact%20Book.pdf

Votel, GEN Joseph L., U.S. Army, commander, U.S. Special Operations Command, statement before the Senate Armed Services Committee, March 26, 2015. As of March 15, 2017:
https://www.armed-services.senate.gov/imo/media/doc/Votel_03-26-15.pdf

————, statement before the House Armed Services Committee Subcommittee on Emerging Threats and Capabilities, March 1, 2016. As of March 15, 2017:
http://docs.house.gov/meetings/AS/AS26/20160301/104552/
HHRG-114-AS26-Wstate-VotelJ-20160301.pdf